Contributing Illustrators: Paula Becker, Anja Boretzki, Jim Bradshaw, Josh Cleland, Garry Colby, Mernie Cole, David Coulson, Mike Dammer, Jack Desrocher, Chuck Dillon, Liz Goulet Dubois, Ana Duna, Leslie Evans, Mar Ferrero, Luke Flowers, Keith Frawley, Patrick Girouard, Peter Grosshauser, Jennifer Harney, Anette Heiberg, Jannie Ho, Jimmy Holder, Paul Hoppe, Deborah Johnson, Anna Jones, Gideon Kendall, Kelly Kennedy, Sue King, Greg Kletsel, Dave Klug, Gary LaCoste, Pat Lewis, Jon Lightle, Steve Mack, Erin Mauterer, Howard McWilliam, Deborah Melmon, Valentina Mendicino, Jo Moon, Julissa Mora, Mike Moran, Mitch Mortimer, Neil Numberman, Bob Ostrom, Jim Paillot, Debbie Palen, Jess Pauwels, Rich Powell, Susan Reagan, Kevin Rechin, Adam Record, Rico Schacherl, Lucy Semple, Jamie Smith, Scott Soeder, Jackie Stafford, Nuno Alexandre Viera, Vin Vogel, Brian Michael Weaver, Brian White, Pete Whitehead, Kevin Zimmer

For information about permission to reprint selections from this book, please contact permissions@highlights.com.

Published by Highlights Press
815 Church Street
Honesdale, Pennsylvania 18431

ISBN: 978-1-63962-087-6
Library of Congress Control Number: 2023935542

Manufactured in Dongguan, Guangdong, China
Mfg. 02/2024

First edition
Visit our website at Highlights.com.

10 9 8 7 6 5 4 3 2

CONTENTS

JANUARY

JANUARY 1
New Year's Day

Knock, knock.

Who's there?

Abby.

Abby who?

Abby new year!

What does the toad say on New Year's Eve?

"Hoppy New Year!"

What comes at the end of New Year's Day?

The letter Y

JANUARY 2
National Science Fiction Day

What do you get when you cross a science-fiction film with a toad?

Star Warts

What's the best kind of book to read when you have a cold?

Sinus fiction

JANUARY 3
Festival of Sleep Day

Why does a bear sleep through the winter?

Would you wake up a bear?

Where do books sleep?
Under their covers

What dinosaur is a good sleeper?

Stego-snore-us

Where can a burger get a great night's sleep?
On a bed of lettuce

What always falls asleep after the table is set?

Napkins

JANUARY 4
National Spaghetti Day

Where does spaghetti go to dance?

The meatball

Why is spaghetti the smartest food?

It always uses its noodle.

What do astronauts like to eat for dinner?

Spaghetti and meteor-balls

JANUARY 5
National Whipped Cream Day

What do monsters put on their ice-cream sundaes?

Whipped scream

JANUARY 6
National Bean Day

How do you make a bean chili?

You send it to the North Pole.

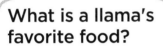
What is a llama's favorite food?
Llama beans

Knock, knock.

Who's there?

Bean.

Bean who?

Bean fishing lately?

What did one burrito say to the other?

"Don't spill the beans!"

JANUARY 7
Old Rock Day

What kind of music do geology students like?

Rock

What is a rock climber's favorite fruit?

Pome-granites

What do geologists say about rocks?

"Never take them for granite."

JANUARY 8
National Bubble Bath Day

Who stole the soap from the bathtub?

The robber ducky

Can Saturn take a bath?

Yes, but it will leave a ring around the tub.

What did the sink say to the bathtub?

"What's soap?"

Where do sheep take a bath?

In a baaa-*thtub*

JANUARY 9
National Apricot Day

Which kind of fruit always carries a bed with it?

An apricot

JANUARY 10
Save the Eagles Day

What does an eagle use to write with?

A bald-point pen

Which kind of bird never needs a haircut?

A bald eagle

JANUARY 11
National Milk Day

How do milk cartons greet each other?

With a milk shake

What gives milk and has a horn?

A milk truck

What do you get from a pampered cow?

Spoiled milk

JANUARY 12
National Pharmacist Day

Where do cows get their medicine?

At the farm-acy

- -

JANUARY 13
National Rubber Ducky Day

National Dress Up Your Pet Day

Does a dog dress more warmly in the summer than in the winter?

Yes, in the winter, a dog wears only a fur coat, but in the summer, a dog wears the same coat and pants.

Where do cats put their dirty clothes?

In the ham-purr

What kind of dog washes clothes?

A laundro-mutt

JANUARY 15
National Bagel Day

How do you keep your bagel from getting stolen?

You put lox on it.

Which kind of bagel can fly?

A plain bagel

Why did the seagull fly over the sea?

Because if it flew over the bay, it'd be a bagel.

JANUARY 16
Appreciate a Dragon Day

What is the greatest honor a dragon can get?

Being voted into the Hall of Flame

What do you get when you cross a dragon and a cheese sandwich?

A grilled cheese sandwich

Knock, knock.

Who's there?

Dragon.

Dragon who?

These jokes are dragon on and on.

JANUARY 17
Kid Inventors Day

What inventions have helped people get up in the world?

The elevator, the escalator, and the alarm clock

Who invented the first airplane that didn't fly?
The Wrong Brothers

What did the robot say to its young inventor?

"You made me what I am today."

JANUARY 18
National Thesaurus Day

What do you call a dinosaur with an extensive vocabulary?

A thesaurus

What is a thesaurus's favorite dessert?

A synonym roll

JANUARY 19
National Popcorn Day

What did the baby corn say to the mama corn?

"Where's popcorn?"

Who is the leader of the popcorn?

The kernel

Penguin Awareness Day

What song do penguins sing on birthdays?

"Freeze a Jolly Good Fellow"

Where do penguins like to go swimming?

The South Pool

Where do penguins get their money?

A snowbank

JANUARY 21
National Squirrel Appreciation Day

What is a squirrel's favorite instrument?

The acorn-dion

Where do squirrels go to school before kindergarten?

Tree school

Why did the squirrel take so long to eat the walnut?

It was one tough nut to crack.

- -

JANUARY 22
National Hot Sauce Day

Why do soccer players like hot sauce?

Because it has a kick to it.

JANUARY 23
Measure Your Feet Day

What do feet say in the theater?

"The shoe must go on."

> ### How do you know when you're upside down?
> *Your feet smell and your nose runs.*

Which figure skater had the biggest skates?

The one with the biggest feet.

How do you put a broken ruler back together again?

Use measuring tape

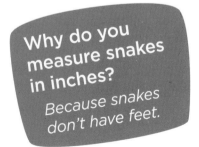

Why do you measure snakes in inches?
Because snakes don't have feet.

JANUARY 24
National Compliment Day

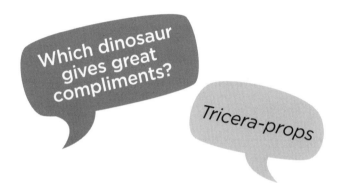

Which dinosaur gives great compliments?

Tricera-props

What did the corn maze say when the scarecrow gave it a compliment?

"Aw shucks, thanks."

Knock, knock.

Who's there?

Tomato.

Tomato who?

I love you from my head tomatoes.

JANUARY 25
National Florida Day

Knock, knock.

Who's there?

Florida.

Florida who?

The Florida bathroom is wet.

Where do pianists go for vacation?

The Florida Keys

Why did the bee go south for the winter?

To visit an ant in Florida

JANUARY 26
Australia Day

What do you get when you cross a kangaroo with an elephant?

Great big holes all over Australia

- -

JANUARY 27
National Chocolate Cake Day

What's the left side of a cake?

The side that has not been eaten

Nancy: This chocolate cake is very rich.
Sheri: Then can I borrow five dollars from it?

JANUARY 28
National LEGO Day

What dinosaur loved playing with blocks?

LEGO-saurus

Boy: Doctor, my LEGO blocks are broken. What do you recommend?

Doctor: Plastic surgery.

Knock, knock.

Who's there?

LEGO.

LEGO who?

LEGO of the doorknob so I can come in!

JANUARY 29
National Puzzle Day

Why didn't the puzzle piece enjoy the party?

It didn't fit in.

What did the tree say when it couldn't solve the puzzle?

"I'm stumped!"

What happened to the man who fell asleep doing a jigsaw puzzle?

He woke up with a puzzled look.

National Croissant Day

What's the opposite of a croissant?

A happy uncle

What did the butter say as it was being spread on the croissant?

"I'm on a roll!"

Backward Day

What is another name for a backward somersault?

A winter-sault

What goes zzub, zzub?
A bee flying backward

How do you spell cat backward?

C-A-T B-A-C-K-W-A-R-D

What do you call a line of rabbits walking backward?

A receding hare line

MORE
JANUARY LAUGHS

What month goes well with peanut butter?

Jam-uary

What is a stinky resolution for the new year?
To bathe less often.

What is a snowman's favorite meat?

Cold cuts

Why should you put your new calendar in the freezer?

To start off the year in a cool way

Will you remember me in a year?

Yes.

Will you remember me in a month?

Yes.

Will you remember me in a week?

Yes.

Knock, knock.

Who's there?

See? You forgot me already!

What happens once in a month, twice in a moment, but never in a hundred years?

The letter M

FEBRUARY

FEBRUARY 1
National Peanut Butter Lovers' Day

Hazel: Why are you dancing on the peanut butter jar?

Oliver: Because it said twist to open.

Knock, knock.

Who's there?

Mammoth.

Mammoth who?

Mammoth is shtuck 'cause I'th been eatin' peanut buther.

What is a skunk's favorite sandwich?
Peanut butter and smelly

What do police officers put on their peanut butter sandwiches?

Traffic jam

FEBRUARY 2
Groundhog Day

What is as big as a groundhog but weighs nothing?

His shadow

What is a groundhog's favorite color?

Mahogany

How do groundhogs greet their parents?

With hogs and kisses

What do you get when you cross a basketball with a groundhog?

Six more weeks of basketball season

FEBRUARY 3
National Golden Retriever Day

What kind of dog plays football?

A golden receiver

- -

FEBRUARY 4
Thank a Mail Carrier Day

What do you get when you cross a dog with an elephant?

A very nervous mail carrier

First mail carrier: A dog licked my leg this morning.

Second mail carrier: Did you put anything on it?

First mail carrier: No, he liked it plain.

FEBRUARY 5
National Weatherperson's Day

What happens when it rains cats and dogs?

You have to be careful not to step in a poodle.

What did the weatherman plant in his garden?

Vine-ripe tornadoes

Knock, knock.

Who's there?

Accordion.

Accordion who?

Accordion to the weather report, it's going to rain tomorrow.

FEBRUARY 6
National Chopsticks Day

What do you call broken chopsticks?
Chopped sticks

What did one chopstick say to the other?

"You're sharp, but please get to the point."

What is another name for a knife?

A chopstick

FEBRUARY 7
National Periodic Table Day

Why are chemistry jokes hard to tell?

They're only good periodically.

I've been trying to write jokes about the periodic table. I'm just not in my element.

What should you do if no one laughs at your chemistry jokes?

Keep trying until you get a reaction.

FEBRUARY 8
Kite Flying Day

Matt: I gave my dad a kite for his birthday.

Marisa: How did he like it?

Matt: He was blown away!

What's a kite's favorite game?

Fly-and-seek

FEBRUARY 9
National Pizza Day

Knock, knock.

Who's there?

Pizza.

Pizza who?

Pizza really nice guy.

What do teachers put on their pizzas?

Graded cheese

FEBRUARY 10
Umbrella Day

Two elephants were under one umbrella. Why didn't they get wet?

It wasn't raining.

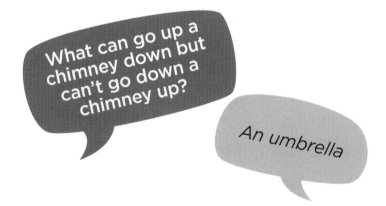

What can go up a chimney down but can't go down a chimney up?

An umbrella

Knock, knock.

Who's there?

Butter.

Butter who?

Butter bring an umbrella—it looks like rain.

FEBRUARY 11
National Guitar Day

What did the guitar say to the musician?

"Stop picking on me!"

Mom: Why did you throw away that guitar?

John: Because it has a hole in the middle.

Derek: Why are you plucking your guitar strings with a pencil?

Joshua: I'm trying to write a song.

- -

FEBRUARY 12
Darwin Day

Knock, knock.

Who's there?

Darwin.

Darwin who?

I'll be Darwin you open the door.

FEBRUARY 13
World Radio Day

Knock, knock.

Who's there?

Turnip.

Turnip who?

Turnip the volume. I can't hear the radio!

What did the television say to the radio?

"You just don't get the picture."

> What can sing and talk but does not have a mouth?
> *An echo*

Knock, knock.

Who's there?

Radio.

Radio who?

Radio not, here I come!

FEBRUARY 14
Valentine's Day

What did the carpet salesman give to his wife for Valentine's Day?

Rugs and kisses

What kind of flower should you not give on Valentine's Day?

Cauliflower

Who did the fish give a valentine to?

His gill-friend

What's the best part about Valentine's Day?

The day after, when all the candy is on sale.

FEBRUARY 15
Hippo Day

What do you call a hippo in a phone booth?

Stuck

What do you call a hippo that never stops eating?

Hippo-bottomless

What does a hippo say when it's cheering?

"Hip-hippo-ray!"

FEBRUARY 16
Do a Grouch a Favor Day

Knock, knock.

Who's there?

Fresno.

Fresno who?

Fresno fun when he's grouchy.

Did you hear about the grouchy neighbor?

Her dog put up a sign that said BEWARE OF OWNER.

- - - - - - - - - - - - - - - - - -

FEBRUARY 17
Random Acts of Kindness Day

A book never written:

How to Be Nice **by Karen N. Sharon**

FEBRUARY 18
National Battery Day

A man walks into a store and asks the clerk for a dead battery. The clerk gets one for him. When the man asks how much it costs, the clerk answers, "No charge."

What keeps bats going?

Batteries

When is a robot like a surgeon?

When it operates on batteries.

FEBRUARY 19
International Tug-of-War Day

What do you get when you play tug-of-war with a pig?

Pulled pork

- - - - - - - - - - - - - - - - - - - -

FEBRUARY 20
National Muffin Day

(Two muffins are in the oven.)

First Muffin: Boy, it's hot in here.

Second Muffin: Wow! A talking muffin!

Knock, knock.

Who's there?

Muffin.

Muffin who?

There's muffin the matter with me—I'm doing fine!

International Mother Language Day

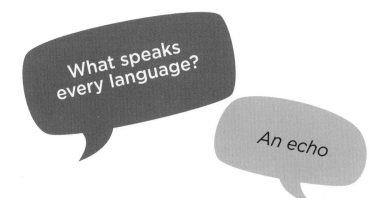

What speaks every language?

An echo

Mother Mouse was taking her children for a stroll. Suddenly, a large cat appeared in their path. Mother Mouse shouted, *"Bow-wow-wow!"* and the cat scurried away.

"You see, my children," Mother Mouse said, "it pays to learn a second language."

FEBRUARY 22
Cook a Sweet Potato Day

What does a sweet potato wear to bed?

Its yam-mies

A sweet potato gave his mother a gift.

As he did, she said to him, "Awww, why are you so sweet?"

He replied, "I guess that's just the way I yam."

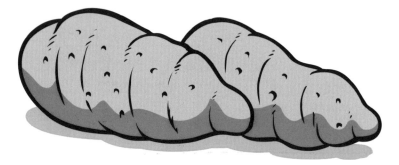

FEBRUARY 23
Play Tennis Day

Why are fish such poor tennis players?

They're afraid of the net.

Why is a tennis court so noisy?

Because everyone raises a racket.

What can you serve but not eat?

A tennis ball

FEBRUARY 24
National Tortilla Chip Day

What is a tortilla chip's favorite kind of dance?

Salsa

What do you call a boat made out of corn?

A tortilla ship

What do ducks like to eat with tortilla chips?

Quack-*amole*

FEBRUARY 25
National Clam Chowder Day

Waiter: Our special today is clams. Would you like to try them?

Diner: Yes, I believe I shell.

Justin: How do you like the clam chowder I made?

Dustin: It's soup-endous!

FEBRUARY 26
Tell a Fairy Tale Day

How do slugs begin their fairy tales?

"Once upon a slime . . ."

Heidi: I really liked the ending to this bunny fairy tale.

Heather: So did I. They all lived hop-pily ever after.

What kind of stories do boats like best?

Ferry tales

FEBRUARY 27
International Polar Bear Day

Where do polar bears vote?
The North Poll

How does a polar bear build its house?
Igloos it together

What do polar bears eat for lunch?
Iceberg-ers

Why do polar bears have fur coats?
Because they would look silly in ski jackets.

FEBRUARY 28
Floral Design Day

How does a tulip ride a bike?

It pedals.

What do flowers say when they explode?

"Ka-bloooom!"

Where do flowers sleep?

In the flower bed

Teacher: Judy, what is your favorite flower?

Judy: A chrysanthemum.

Teacher: Spell it.

Judy: I changed my mind. I like roses much better.

What did the little ghost give her mom for her birthday?

A boo-quet of flowers

FEBRUARY 29
Leap Day

When do kangaroos celebrate their birthdays?

During leap year

My friend is ten years old, but she has only had three birthdays. How can that be?

She was born on February 29 in a leap year.

MORE
FEBRUARY LAUGHS

What is Spider-Man's favorite month?

Web-ruary

What falls in winter but never gets hurt?

Snow

What month has the best coffee?

Feb-BREW-ary

> **Can February March?**
> *No, but April May.*

Knock, knock.
  Who's there?
Scold.
  Scold who?
May I come in? Scold outside!

MARCH

MARCH 1
National Pig Day

What did the doctor give the pig for its rash?

Oink-*ment*

What do you call a pig that does karate?
A pork chop

What do pigs do when they play basketball?

They hog the ball.

MARCH 2
Read Across America Day

What does Teacher Rabbit read to her bunnies?

Hare-raising stories

Where do scientists read facts about volcanoes?

In magma-zines

MARCH 3
National Cold Cuts Day

Pam: Did you hear about the man who kept bandages in the refrigerator?

Sam: No. Why did he do that?

Pam: In case he got any cold cuts.

MARCH 4
National Marching Band Day

Who leads the bird band?

The con-duck-tor

What's big and gray with horns?

An elephant marching band

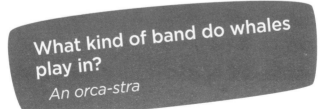

Knock, knock.

Who's there?

Abandon.

Abandon who?

Abandon the street is marching this way.

What kind of band do whales play in?

An orca-stra

MARCH 5
Reel Film Day

What did the director say when she finished filming a mummy scene?

"That's a wrap!"

Two goats found a roll of film and began to eat it.

Goat 1: How do you like it?

Goat 2: Not bad, but I liked the book better.

MARCH 6
National Dentist's Day

What's the best time to go to the dentist?

Tooth-hurty

Why did the queen go to the dentist?

To get her teeth crowned

Why did the doughnut go to the dentist?

To get a chocolate filling

MARCH 7
National Cereal Day

What is a cereal's favorite kind of music?

Snap-crackle pop

Knock, knock.

Who's there?

Cereal.

Cereal who?

Cereal pleasure to meet you!

MARCH 8
National Proofreading Day

Kyle: I got one wrong on my spelling test. Oh well, no one knows how to spell everything.

Emma: I do! E-V-E-R-Y-T-H-I-N-G.

What do witches love about their computers?

The spell-checker

What word do even teachers spell wrong?

Wrong

MARCH 9
National Meatball Day

Jackson: Let me guess what you had for lunch today. You had spaghetti with meatballs and mashed potatoes.

Mackenzie: Wow! That's amazing. Did you read my mind?

Jackson: No, your chin.

Why do meatballs make good storybook characters?

They are well-rounded.

What did the father meatball say to his sleepy child?

"It's pasta your bedtime."

MARCH 10
National Pack Your Lunch Day

Leo: I packed my own lunch today.

Kelly: What did you bring?

Leo: Uh . . . chocolate soup.

Kelly: Chocolate soup?

Leo: Well, this morning it was ice cream.

What did the caveman pack for lunch?

A club sandwich

What did the shark pack for lunch?

A corned-reef sandwich

MARCH 11
National Worship of Tools Day

What tools do you need for math?

Multi-pliers

What type of tool does a prehistoric reptile carpenter use?

A dino-saw

What tools did the Three Little Pigs use to build their houses?

Hammers

What kind of tool do you need to fix a broken ape?

A monkey wrench

National Plant a Flower Day

What is a frog's favorite flower?

A croak-us

Where do flowers go to school?

To the kinder-garden

What is the fiercest flower to plant?

A tiger lily

What are the saddest flowers?

Cry-santhemums

What flower does everyone have?

Tulips

MARCH 13
National Jewel Day

What's the difference between a jeweler and a biologist?

One sells the watches, and the other watches the cells.

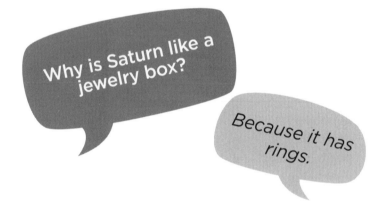

What did the rabbit give to his wife for her birthday?

A 14-carrot necklace

MARCH 14
Pi Day

Mae: I couldn't finish the book about pi.
Savanna: Why not?
Mae: It kept going on forever.

What is a math teacher's favorite ice-cream flavor?

Pi-stachio

What do Spanish mathematicians eat?

Pi-ella

What do you get when you divide the circumference of a jack-o'-lantern by its diameter?

Pumpkin pi

MARCH 15
National Shoe The World Day

What are a plumber's favorite shoes?

Clogs

What shoes do spies wear?

Sneakers

What do you call shoes made out of a banana?

Slippers

Why was the father caterpillar upset?

Because all of his kids needed new shoes.

MARCH 16
National Panda Day

What's black-and-white and black-and-white and black-and-white?

A panda rolling down a hill

What scares pandas?

Bam-BOO!

Why do pandas like old movies?

Because they're in black and white.

What do Asian bears eat for breakfast?

Panda-cakes

MARCH 17
Saint Patrick's Day

Knock, knock.

Who's there?

Irish.

Irish who?

Irish you a happy Saint Patrick's Day!

What do you call a fake Irish stone?

A shamrock

MARCH 18
National Sloppy Joe Day

What do you call a messy baby kangaroo?

A sloppy joey

MARCH 19
National Let's Laugh Day

How do you make ice laugh?
You just pour water on it, and it cracks up.

Do you know how to make a hamburger laugh?
You pickle it.

How do you make a squid laugh?
With ten-tickles

How do you make an orange laugh?
Tickle its navel.

Where do comedians go for lunch?
The laugh-eteria

What do elephants do for laughs?
They tell people jokes.

MARCH 20
World Frog Day

What happened to the frog that parked illegally?

He got toad.

> ### Where do frogs take notes?
> *On lily pads*

What did the frog order for lunch?

French flies and a large croak

Why did the frog go to the hospital?

It needed a hop-eration.

Why do frogs make good outfielders?

Because they never miss a fly.

MARCH 21
World Poetry Day

What hand is best to write poetry with?

Neither—you should use a pencil!

What kind of tree has poems on it?

A poetry

What do you call a poem recited by a chicken?

Poultry

How do poets say hello?
"Hey, haven't we metaphor?"

MARCH 22
International Day of the Seal

What lives in the ocean and always agrees with you?

A seal of approval

What animals are found on legal documents?

Seals

A girl opened a box of animal crackers and took one out. She said, "Mom, should we eat these? The seal is broken!"

What did the seal say when it got stuck in seaweed?

"Kelp!"

MARCH 23
National Puppy Day

What animal has the head of a dog, the tail of a dog, and barks like a dog, but isn't a dog?

A puppy

What did the puppy say when asked if it was in school yet?

"Yes, I'm in pre-K-9."

Why are dalmatian puppies so bad at playing hide-and-seek?

Because they're always spotted.

- -

MARCH 24
National Cheesesteak Day

What's a female horse's favorite sandwich?

A filly cheesesteak

MARCH 25
International Waffle Day

Knock, knock.

Who's there?

Waffle.

Waffle who?

It's waffle that you still haven't opened the door!

What did the syrup say to its long-lost friend?

"It's been a waffle long time!"

- -

MARCH 26
National Spinach Day

Father: Eat your spinach, son. It will put color in your cheeks.

Son: But I don't want green cheeks!

What is a Hula-Hoop's favorite vegetable?

Spinach

MARCH 27
World Theater Day

Where do soccer players like to sit in a theater?

In the ball-cony

What do feet say in the theater?

"The shoe must go on."

MARCH 28
National Something on a Stick Day

What is a librarian's favorite food?

Shush-kabob

Why was the candy apple so excited?

He was going to see his Granny Smith.

MARCH 29
International Mermaid Day

What do mermaids wear in a car?

Sea belts

How does a mermaid text a friend?

On her shell phone

MARCH 30
National Pencil Day

What's the biggest pencil in the world?

Pennsylvania

Why shouldn't you write with a broken pencil?

It's pointless.

What happened when the pigpen broke?

The pig had to use a pencil.

What did the cowboy say to the pencil?

"Draw, pardner!"

MARCH 31
National Crayon Day

What is the only finger you can put in a box of crayons?

Your pinky

What kind of berry loves to color?

Crayon-berries

MORE
MARCH LAUGHS

How far is it from March to June?

Just a short spring

What's the best month for a parade?

March

What did the tree say when spring came?

"What a re-leaf!"

How is the letter *A* like a flower?

They both have a bee coming after them.

Veronica: Why are you washing your trampoline?

Charlie: It was time for some spring cleaning.

APRIL

APRIL 1
April Fools' Day

What monster plays the most April Fools' jokes?

Prank-enstein

Why do eggs like April Fools' day?
They love practical yolks.

Why is everyone so tired on April Fools' day?

Because they just finished a 31-day March.

What do ghosts say on April 1?

April Ghouls!

APRIL 2
National Peanut Butter and Jelly Day

What do you wear when you're eating a peanut butter and jelly sandwich?

Jammies

What has sharp fangs and sticks to the roof of your mouth?

A peanut butter and Jeholopterus sandwich

A book never written:

***PB & J Lunches* by Sammy Chez**

Did you hear the joke about peanut butter and jelly?

I did, but I don't want to spread it.

National Find a Rainbow Day

What is at the end of a rainbow?

The letter W

What kind of bow can't be tied?

A rainbow

How did the rainbow do on the science test?

It passed with flying colors.

What do storm clouds wear in their hair?

Rainbows

What do you call a rainbow without any colors?

A plain-bow

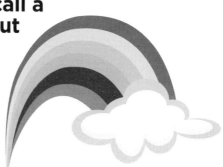

APRIL 4
International Carrot Day

How do you know that carrots are good for your eyes?

Have you ever seen a rabbit wearing glasses?

What did one snowman say to the other?

"Do you smell carrots?"

What's the difference between a unicorn and a carrot?

One is a funny beast, and one is a bunny feast.

What's orange and sounds like a parrot?

A carrot

APRIL 5
National Dandelion Day

What do you get when you cross a dog and a dandelion?

A collie-flower

When is a well-dressed lion like a weed?

When he's a dandelion

Where are dandelions on windy days?

Everywhere

APRIL 6
National Student Athlete Day

What do you call an athletic student pumpkin?

A jock-o'-lantern

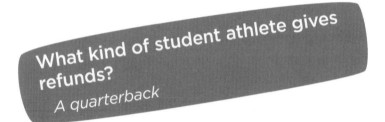

What kind of student athlete gives refunds?

A quarterback

Where do student athletes go to get new uniforms?

New Jersey

Manuel: Are there any athletes in your family?

Maria: My brother has been swimming for five years.

Manuel: He must be pretty tired.

APRIL 7
National Beaver Day

What do beavers eat for breakfast?

Oak-meal

What did the beaver say to the tree?

"It was nice gnawing you!"

How did the beaver get onto the website?

He logged on.

APRIL 8
National Zoo Lovers' Day

Why don't you see many chipmunks in zoos?

Because they can't afford a ticket.

Why couldn't anyone call the zoo?

All the phone lions were busy.

What are the zoo's floors made of?

Reptiles

Knock, knock.

Who's there?

Census.

Census who?

Census Saturday, let's go to the zoo.

APRIL 9
National Unicorn Day

What street do unicorns live on?

Mane Street

How do unicorns wrap presents?
With a rainbow

Why do unicorns like silly jokes?

Because they're uni-corny.

Why are unicorns good at volleyball?

They know how to spike the ball.

APRIL 10
National Golfer's Day

Why did the golfer wear two pairs of pants?

In case he got a hole in one.

Why don't golfers usually drink coffee?

They always carry tees.

What do you get when you cross a golfer with a librarian?

Book clubs

What is a golfer's favorite dinosaur?

Tee rex

APRIL 11
National Submarine Day

What do sardines call a submarine?

A can of people

What is a submarine's favorite game?

Hide-and-sink

Why did the submarine quit its job?

It was under too much pressure.

Big Wind Day

Why do skeletons get sick on windy days?

The wind goes right through them.

What color is the wind?

Blew

What did the tree say to the wind?

"Leaf me alone."

When are your eyes not eyes?

When the winter wind makes them water.

APRIL 13
Thomas Jefferson Day

What did Thomas Jefferson put up for every holiday?

The Decoration of Independence

APRIL 14
National Dolphin Day

Why did the dolphin cross the ocean?

To get to the other tide

Why do dolphins live in salt water?

Because pepper water makes them sneeze.

What did the shark say when he bumped into the dolphin?

"I didn't do it on porpoise."

APRIL 15
National Laundry Day

Where do witches go to wash their clothes?

The laundry broom

What happened to the shirt that got destroyed in the wash?

It was a casual tee.

What animal hates to do laundry?

A leopard, because it has so many spots.

What did the washing machine say to the dryer after doing laundry?

"Get a load of this!"

National Librarian Day

What do librarians use as bait when they go fishing?

Bookworms

What is a librarian's favorite prehistoric creature?

A pterodactyl, because the P is always silent.

Bat Appreciation Day

What do bats do for exercise?

Acrobatics

What do bats do for fun?

They like to hang out with their friends.

How do baby bats learn how to fly?

They just wing it.

APRIL 18
National *Velociraptor* Awareness Day

Which dinosaur wrapped Christmas presents the fastest?

The Veloci-wrapper

Which dinosaur was the most musical?

The Veloci-rapper

What's the best way to talk to a *Velociraptor*?

Long distance

APRIL 19
National Garlic Day

Did you hear about the dog who ate a bunch of garlic?

His bark was worse than his bite.

APRIL 20
National High Five Day

Which tree gives the best high fives?

A palm tree

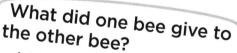

What did one bee give to the other bee?

A high hive

APRIL 21
National Bulldogs Are Beautiful Day

What kind of dog chases anything that's red?

A bulldog

Brenda: Stop making faces at that bulldog.

Nicole: Well, he started it!

APRIL 22
Earth Day

Teacher: Why shouldn't people litter?

Jayden: Because it's bad for Earth—literally!

Which U.S. president liked the environment the most?

Tree-adore Roosevelt

APRIL 23
World Laboratory Day

Why was there thunder and lightning in the science lab?

The scientists were brainstorming.

Which type of dog loves science?

A labrador

APRIL 24
National Skipping Day

Meira: Have you heard the joke about the jump rope?

Eli: No. Tell me.

Meira: Skip it!

APRIL 25
National DNA Day

Why does DNA have no fashion sense?

It always wears the same old genes.

Doctor: My tests show that your DNA is backward.

Me: . . . AND?

Why did the DNA put on mascara?

It was part of its genetic makeup.

National Pretzel Day

What is a pretzel's favorite dance?

The Twist

Why are pretzels called pretzels?

Because they are knot-bread.

What did the pretzel twist say to the pretzel rod?

"I'd rather knot."

APRIL 27
Morse Code Day

What goes *dot-dot-croak, dot-dash-croak*?

Morse toad

Why did the telegraph operator refuse to send the message again?

He had no remorse.

Why did Dot go in such a hurry?

She was late and had to dash.

APRIL 28
National Superhero Day

What do you call a computer superhero?

A screen saver

Where do superheroes shop?

At the supermarket

Who helps a soccer superhero?

A sidekick

Why did the superhero save the pickle?

Because he wanted to eat it later.

APRIL 29
International Dance Day

Where do computers go to dance?

The disco

> What dance do eggs like best?
> *The Yolky Pokey*

What's a vampire's favorite dance?

The fang-dango

What is a detective's favorite dance?

The evi-dance

Where did people dance in medieval times?

In knight clubs

International Jazz Day

Why do farmers play soft jazz for their corn stalks?

It's easy on the ears.

MORE APRIL LAUGHS

Which month did the *Mayflower* come to America?

In April. April showers bring May flowers.

What is a circle's favorite month?

Shape-ril

Why is April the smartest month?

It can never be fooled.

> **When do gorillas fall from the sky?**
> *During Ape-ril showers*

When is a frog's favorite time to jump?

Spring

What is spring's favorite kind of pickles?

Daffo-dills

MAY 1
Save the Rhino Day

How do you stop a rhinoceros from charging?

You unplug it.

What is a rhinoceros horn made of?

Rhinestone

What's the difference between an African rhino and an Indian rhino?

About three thousand miles

MAY 2
National Baby Day

What do babies ride at amusement parks?

Stroller coasters

How do you get an astronaut's baby to fall asleep?

You rocket

What's the difference between a coat and a baby?

A coat is what you wear. A baby is what you were.

When are babies good at basketball?

When they're dribbling.

How many men were born in 1996?

No men were born—only babies.

MAY 3
International Wild Koala Day

How does a koala stop a movie?

She presses the paws button.

> **What's a koala's favorite drink?**
> *Coca-Koala*

Why couldn't the marsupial get a job?

He wasn't koala-fied.

Where do koalas go most frequently?

To sleep

MAY 4
Star Wars Day

How do Star Wars fans greet each other today?

"May the Fourth be with you!"

Why is Yoda so good at gardening?

Because he has a green thumb.

What do you call small potatoes that have turned to the dark side?

Vader Tots

> **What does Obi-Wan Kenobi order at an Italian restaurant?**
>
> *Only-one-cannoli*

Knock, knock.

Who's there?

Yoda.

Yoda who?

Yoda man! Let's hang out some more.

MAY 5
Cinco de Mayo

What is the shortest food to serve on Cinco de Mayo?

Inch-iladas

Mateo: Did everyone like your piñata at your Cinco de Mayo party?

Marisol: It was a big hit!

MAY 6
National Nurses Day

Patient: Nurse, Nurse! I was playing my harmonica, and I swallowed it.

Nurse: You're lucky you weren't playing a piano!

Nurse: May I take your pulse?

Patient: Why? Haven't you got one of your own?

MAY 7
National Tourism Day

What is green and has a trunk?

A seasick tourist

Tourist: Look! A bunch of cows.

Cowboy: Not bunch—herd.

Tourist: Heard what?

Cowboy: Herd of cows.

Tourist: Sure, I've heard of cows.

Cowboy: No, a cow herd.

Tourist: That's OK. I have no secrets to keep from cows!

MAY 8
World Donkey Day

What kind of key can't open a door?

A donkey

What do you call a teeter-totter for donkeys?

A hee-haw *seesaw*

Where does a donkey go on a field trip?

A mule-seum

What do you call a donkey that's cold?

Brrr-*o!*

MAY 9
Lost Sock Memorial Day

What does a lost sock look for?

Its sole mate

Where does a sock go when it loses its partner?

To the repair shop

MAY 10
National Clean Your Room Day

Blake: Dad, would you ever scold me for something I didn't do?

Dad: Of course I wouldn't, Blake. Why do you ask?

Blake: I was just wondering because I didn't clean my room.

How did the astronaut's mom know he didn't clean his room?

There was a lot of stardust everywhere.

National Eat What You Want Day

What do birds eat for dessert?

Chocolate-chirp *cookies*

What does a sea monster eat for dinner?

Fish and ships

What do you call a cat that eats lemons?

A sourpuss

Why did the monkey eat so many bananas?

He liked them a bunch.

What did the gorilla eat before dinner?

An ape-etizer

MAY 12
National Odometer Day

What was the turtle doing on the highway?

One mile per hour

Police officer: I'm giving you a ticket for driving eighty-five miles per hour.

Driver: But I've only been driving for fifteen minutes!

- -

MAY 13
Leprechaun Day

What is a leprechaun's favorite type of music?

Shamrock 'n' roll

> **What do you call a leprechaun at the North Pole?**
>
> *Lost*

MAY 14
Chicken Dance Day

How do chickens dance?

Chick to chick

Diner: Look at this chicken. One leg is longer than the other.

Waitress: Are you going to eat it or dance with it?

MAY 15
Dinosaur Day

What do you call a dinosaur wearing a cowboy hat?

Tyrannosaurus Tex

What does a *Triceratops* sit on?
Its Tricera-bottom

What was the scariest prehistoric animal?

The terror-dactyl

What do you get if you give a dinosaur a pogo stick?

Big holes in your driveway

What do you call a sleeping prehistoric reptile?

A dino-snore

MAY 16
National Love a Tree Day

What did the tree wear to the pool party?

Swimming trunks

How do trees get on the computer?
They log in.

What type of dog has a silent bark?

A dogwood

How did the oak get lost?

It took the wrong root.

Which type of tree is most likely to feel really ill?

A sycamore

MAY 17
World Baking Day

What does a gorilla wear while baking?

An ape-ron

What does bread do when it is baked with shoe polish?

It rises and shines.

Why did the baker bake some bread?

He kneaded a snack.

Why does the baseball fan bake cakes?

Because he likes to watch the batter.

MAY 18
International Museum Day

Why do museums have old dinosaur bones?

They can't afford new ones.

- -

MAY 19
May Ray Day

How do you know the sun is smart?

It's so bright.

What did the comet say to the sun?

See you next time around!

Why didn't the sun go to college?

Because it already had thousands of degrees.

What holds the sun up in the sky?

Sunbeams

National Pick Strawberries Day

What is a scarecrow's favorite fruit?

Strawberries

How do you mend a broken strawberry?

With a strawberry patch

Why are strawberries such unlucky drivers?

They always get stuck in a jam.

MAY 21
National Waitstaff Day

What is the waiter's favorite sport?

Tennis, because they serve so well.

Diner: What is this fly doing on my ice cream?

Waiter: I believe it's downhill skiing, sir.

Diner: Waiter, I'm in a hurry. Will the pancakes be long?

Waiter: No, they'll be round.

Diner: Do you serve crabs?

Waiter: Yes, we serve anyone.

MAY 22
National Buy a Musical Instrument Day

What did the conductor say to the band when they misbehaved?

"Compose yourselves!"

> **What did the violin say to the viola when they met?**
>
> *"Cello!"*

What do brass instruments wear in the ocean?

Tuba gear

What is a trombone's favorite thing to do on the playground?

The slide

MAY 23
World Turtle Day

What is a turtle's favorite thing to wear in the winter?

A turtleneck

What do you get when you cross a porcupine with a turtle?

A slowpoke

Why is the turtle the strongest creature in the world?

It carries its house on its back.

MAY 24
National Escargot Day

Snail: Hi, I'd like to buy a car.

Car salesperson: Uhh . . . sure. What kind of car?

Snail: I'd like a car with *S*'s painted all over it.

Car salesperson: Why?

Snail: I want people to say, "Look at that *S*-car go!"

- -

MAY 25
Towel Day

What gets wetter the more it dries?

A towel

What dip do bath towels eat at parties?
Shower cream and onion

MAY 26
Dracula Day

Why did Dracula go to the doctor?

He was coffin.

Where does Dracula go first when he visits New York?

The Vampire State Building

Which flavor of ice cream is Dracula's favorite?

Vein-illa

MAY 27
National Sunscreen Day

What do you call a pig who forgot to apply sunscreen?

Bacon

Why do bananas wear sunscreen?

So they don't peel.

MAY 28
Slug
Appreciation Day

What did the slug say when she left the party?

See you next slime!

What is a slug's favorite mode of transportation?

A snail-boat

- -

MAY 29
National Paper
Clip Day

What did the paper clip say to the magnet?

"You're so attractive!"

MAY 30
National Water a Flower Day

Janelle: Where are you going with that watering can?

Jamal: Out to water my flowers.

Janelle: But it's raining.

Jamal: OK, I'll wear my raincoat.

- - - - - - - - - - - - - - - - - - - -

MAY 31
International Flight Attendant Day

Passenger on plane: Those people down there look like ants!

Flight attendant: They are ants. We haven't left the ground yet.

MORE
MAY LAUGHS

What is the shortest month?

May—it only has three letters.

Which month is in charge of the year?
The May-or

Which month is easiest to get lost in?

May-ze

START

FINISH

Knock, knock.

Who's there?

May.

May who?

Maybe could you open this door?

What do you call a meadow of flowers?

A pollen-nation

Which state loves May the most?

May-ne

Johnny's mother had three children. The first child was named April. The second was named May. What was the third child's name?

Johnny

JUNE

JUNE 1
World Milk Day

What do ghosts drink?

Evaporated milk

> ### Why was the cat so small?
> *Because she only drank condensed milk.*

Why is milk the fastest liquid?

It's pasteurized before you even see it.

How do you keep milk from getting sour?

You leave it in the cow.

JUNE 2
National Rocky Road Day

What flavor of ice cream do drivers like the least?

Rocky road

How did the ice-cream truck get a flat tire?

It was on a rocky road.

What did the shop owner say when he accidentally doubled an order of chocolate and marshmallows?

We've got a rocky road ahead of us.

JUNE 3
World Bicycle Day

Why couldn't the bicycle stand up by itself?

It was two tired.

Why couldn't the dinosaur ride the bicycle?

Because it didn't have a thumb to ring the bell.

What do flowers and bicycles have in common?

Petals

JUNE 4
National Cheese Day

What do you call a cheese that talks too much?

A cheddar box

What kind of cheese is made backward?

Edam

What kind of cheese do you find in the sea?

Manta ray jack

Hot-Air Balloon Day

What music should you avoid at a hot-air balloon festival?

Pop

Which monkey can float in the sky?

A hot-air baboon

JUNE 6
National Yo-Yo Day

What do you call a yo-yo without a string?

A no-yo

What kind of toy likes to rap?

A yo! yo!

What's it like to be a yo-yo champ?

It has its ups and downs.

- -

JUNE 7
National Boone Day

How many ears does Daniel Boone have?

Three: a right ear, a left ear, and a frontier

JUNE 8
National Best Friends Day

What did the watermelon say to its best friend?

"You're one in a melon!"

Who are your tongue's best friends?
Your taste buds

Why do ghosts and vampires get along?

Because vampires are a ghoul's best friend.

Who is your best friend at school?
Your principal

JUNE 9
National Donald Duck Day

What did Donald Duck say when he dropped the dishes?

"I hope I didn't quack any!"

What did Donald Duck wear to the fancy party?

A ducks-edo

When does Donald Duck wake up?

At the quack of dawn.

What is Donald Duck's favorite meal?

Soup and quack-ers

JUNE 10
National Herbs and Spices Day

What do you call an elderly herb merchant?

An old thyme-r

What do you say when you give someone a set of spices for Christmas?

"Seasonings greetings!"

Which spice is always in trouble?

Cinnamon, because it's always grounded.

What's green and sings?

Elvis Parsley

Knock, knock.

Who's there?

Cumin.

Cumin who?

Cumin side—it's freezing out there!

JUNE 11
National Corn on the Cob Day

What does corn get if you leave it in the barn too long?

Cobwebs

First Corncob: You're invited to my birthday party!

Second Corncob: A-maize-ing! Thanks!

For which vegetable do you throw away the outside, cook the inside, eat the outside, and throw away the inside?

Corn on the cob

JUNE 12
Superman Day

What do you call a chicken who thinks he's Superman?

Cluck Kent

> Why is Superman's costume so tight?
>
> *Because he wears a size S.*

- -

JUNE 13
National Weed Your Garden Day

Why do gardeners hate weeds?

If you give them an inch, they'll take a yard.

What kind of weed does not grow in a garden?

Seaweed

JUNE 14
Flag Day

Pat: I once sang "The Star-Spangled Banner" for three hours nonstop.

Shannon: That's nothing. I can sing "The Stars and Stripes Forever."

JUNE 15
National Photography Day

Clara: How did your photo of the barley field turn out?

Max: Pretty grainy.

> **What's a photographer's favorite kind of sandwich?**
>
> *Cheese*

National Flip-Flop Day

Why can't cows wear flip-flops?

Because they lactose.

What do you call someone who can't turn flapjacks?

A flip-flop

Did you hear about the man with two left feet who went into the shoe store?

He asked the salesman, "Do you have any flip-flips?"

National Eat Your Vegetables Day

Which vegetable lives at the zoo?

Zucchini

What is a kayaker's least favorite vegetable?

A leek

Where do vegetables read the news?

News-peppers

Patient: Are carrots healthy?

Doctor: I've never heard one complain.

JUNE 18
National Go Fishing Day

Why do people go fishing early in the morning?

Because they want to catch break-fish.

Why did the astronomer go fishing at midnight?

Because that's the best time to catch a starfish.

JUNE 19
Juneteenth

What did one Juneteenth Flag say to the other?

Nothing. It just waved.

JUNE 20
Ice-Cream Soda Day

What is the best thing to put into an ice-cream soda?

A straw

Knock, knock.

Who's there?

Ice-cream soda.

Ice-cream soda who?

Ice-cream soda whole world can hear me!

JUNE 21
World Giraffe Day

What do you get when two giraffes collide?

A giraffe-ic jam

Why don't giraffes ever learn to swim?

Because it's easier for them just to walk on the bottom of the pool.

> ### Why do giraffes have long necks?
> *Because their feet smell!*

What is worse than a centipede with sore feet?

A giraffe with a sore throat

JUNE 22
National Onion Rings Day

What do you call a hobbit who likes fried food?

Lord of the Onion Rings

Why did Mr. Potato Head carry a cell phone?

In case Mr. Onion rings

Why did the woman cry after her boyfriend proposed?

He proposed with an onion ring.

JUNE 23
National Pink Flamingo Day

Why are flamingo children spoiled?

Their parents don't put their foot down.

Why does a flamingo stand on one leg?

If it lifted both legs, it would fall over!

JUNE 24
International Fairy Day

Who is the smartest fairy in Neverland?

Thinker-bell

JUNE 25
National Catfish Day

What is stranger than seeing a catfish?

Seeing a fishbowl

What kind of fish chases mice?

A catfish

What party game do catfish like to play?

Salmon Says

JUNE 26
National Canoe Day

How does a tiger paddle a canoe?

He uses his roar.

What is the best color for a canoe?

Oar-ange

What did one camper say to the other?

I can row a boat, canoe?

JUNE 27
National Sunglasses Day

What does Tarzan say when he sees a herd of elephants wearing sunglasses?

Nothing—he doesn't recognize them.

How did the astronaut serve lemonade?

In sunglasses

Why did the teacher wear sunglasses?

Because her students were so bright.

JUNE 28
National Alaska Day

Knock, knock.

Who's there?

Alaska.

Alaska who?

Alaska my parents if I can go sledding!

What is the capital of Alaska?

Come on— Juneau this one!

Where is the best place in Alaska to dock your boat?

Anchorage

JUNE 29
International Mud Day

Knock, knock.

Who's there?

Butternut.

Butternut who?

Butternut let me in—my feet are muddy.

What do you call a frog who's stuck in the mud?

Un-hoppy

JUNE 30
International Asteroid Day

How do astronauts keep their pants up?

They wear asteroid belts.

What did the black hole say after it swallowed an asteroid?

"It was good, but I wish it had been a little meteor."

Why wouldn't the asteroid get married?

It was afraid of comet-ment.

MORE JUNE LAUGHS

Do fish go on summer vacation?

No, because they're always in school.

Hazel: Today is the summer solstice!

Matt: I have a feeling it's going to be a long day.

Knock, knock.

Who's there?

June.

June who?

June know how long I've been standing out here knocking?

Dana: You know what bugs me about June?

Dan: What?

Dana: June bugs.

What did the beach say when the tide came in?

Long time, no sea.

Why are mountains the funniest place to go on vacation?

Because they are hill-arious

JULY

JULY 1
International Joke Day

Why should you never tell a joke while ice-skating?

Because the ice will crack up.

Why can't you tell a joke to a snake?

Because you can't pull its leg.

What happened when the boxer told a joke?

He hit the punch line.

JULY 2
World UFO Day

What did the astronaut see in her frying pan?

An unidentified frying object

Where did the alien put her teacup?

On a flying saucer

What do space aliens eat for breakfast?

Flying sausages

JULY 3
National Fried Clam Day

What do you call a fried clam that blends in with its surroundings?

Clam-ouflaged

JULY 4
Independence Day

Mr. Smith: Do you have the Fourth of July in England?

Lord Smythe: Yes. We also have the second and third of July.

Where was the Declaration of Independence signed?

At the bottom

What was the most popular dance in 1776?

Indepen-dance

JULY 5
National Hawai'i Day

What has two eyes but cannot see?

Hawai'i

What do you call a Hawai'ian celebration?

A hula-day

JULY 6
National Umbrella Cover Day

When is a new umbrella old?

When it is used up.

> **What goes up when rain comes down?**
> *An umbrella*

If it's raining and everyone has the same kind of umbrella, what kind is it?

Wet

Tell the Truth Day

Which instrument never tells the truth?

A lyre

Why did the skeleton always tell the truth?

He wanted tibia honest.

Teacher: Leah, you missed school yesterday.

Leah: Well, to tell you the truth, I didn't miss it that much.

JULY 8
Math 2.0 Day

Alex: Did you know that 10+10 is the same answer as 11+11?

Rose: You need to check your math.

Alex: It's true! 10+10 is 20. And 11+11 is 22.

In mathematics, what is The Law of the Doughnut?

Two halves make a hole

Why was the math book sad?

Because it had too many problems.

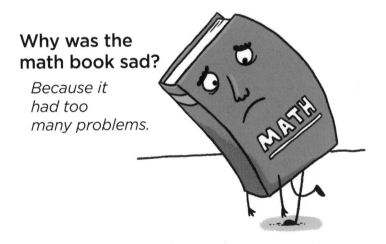

Why are cowboys bad at math?

They're always rounding things up.

JULY 9
National Sugar Cookie Day

Why did the sugar cookie go to the doctor?

It felt crumby.

Why did the girl put sugar cookies under her pillow?
She wanted to have sweet dreams.

How does the queen like her sugar cookies?

Decorated with royal icing

JULY 10
National Kitten Day

What did the young cat say after telling a funny joke?

"I'm just kitten."

What do kittens call their fathers?

Paw

What do you call a pile of kittens?

A meow-*tain*

What do you call a kitten after it's six months old?

Seven months old

National Swimming Pool Day

Why can't two elephants go into the same swimming pool at the same time?

Because they have only one pair of trunks.

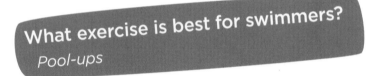

What exercise is best for swimmers?

Pool-ups

Where do automobiles go swimming?

In a carpool.

Knock, knock.

Who's there?

Philip.

Philip who?

Philip your pool. I want to go swimming!

JULY 12
National
Pecan Pie Day

What is a woodpecker's favorite food?

Peck-on pie.

- -

JULY 13
National
French Fry Day

Why did the potato go to France?

It wanted to be a french fry.

> **Where do french fries go on vacation?**
> *Greece*

What do you call french fries on the moon?

Crater taters

JULY 14
Shark Awareness Day

What sharks would you find at a construction site?

Hammerhead sharks

What does the tooth fairy bring to a shark that has lost a tooth?

A sand dollar.

> **What do you get when you cross a snowman and a shark?**
>
> *Frostbite*

Imagine you are in a rowboat and you're being chased by a shark. What is the best way to escape?

Stop imagining!

JULY 15
I Love Horses Day

What do horses do at bedtime?

They hit the hay.

> **What kind of horse does the bogeyman ride?**
>
> *A nightmare*

What do horses put on their burgers?

Mayo-neighs

Why did the horse eat with his mouth open?
He had bad stable manners.

What does it mean when you find a horseshoe?

Some poor horse is walking around in just his socks.

JULY 16
World
Snake Day

What did the snake say to his little sister?

"Stop being such a rattle-tail!"

> ### What type of snake builds things?
> *A boa constructor*

What kind of snake is good to have on a car?

A windshield viper

JULY 17
World Emoji Day

What is a cow emoji called?

An e-moo-ji

What does an emoji say before it takes a photo?

"Smiley!"

JULY 18
World Listening Day

What did the robot say to the gas pump?

"Take your finger out of your ear and listen to me!"

JULY 19
Stick Out Your Tongue Day

What did the sandal say to the sneaker?

"Don't stick your tongue out at me!"

JULY 20
International Chess Day

Why didn't the tree play checkers?

It's a chess-nut.

What do chess players have for breakfast?

Pawn-cakes

What do you call a person who is learning to play chess?

A rook rookie

Invite an Alien to Live with You Day

Why don't aliens have to clean up after themselves?

Because space is a vacuum.

When you bump into a three-headed alien, what should you say?

"Excuse me, excuse me, excuse me!"

What did the alien say to your cat?

"Take me to your litter."

JULY 22
National Hammock Day

Where do pigs like to nap?

Hammocks

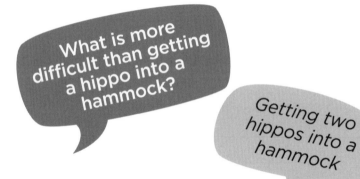

What is more difficult than getting a hippo into a hammock?

Getting two hippos into a hammock

What kind of music do hammocks like?

Rock

Why did Harriet put up a hammock between two walls in her home?

It really tied the room together.

JULY 23
"Hot Enough For Ya?" Day

What's the best kind of letter to read on a hot day?

Fan mail

Daughter: It's so hot today. Could you please tell me a ghost story?

Dad: Sure, but why?

Daughter: Because ghost stories are so chilling.

JULY 24
National Tell an Old Joke Day

Why did the chicken cross the road?

To get to the other side

Why did the boy throw the butter out the window?

He wanted to see butterfly.

What's black and white and red all over?

A sunburned zebra

Knock, knock.

Who's there?

Boo.

Boo who?

Don't cry! It's just a joke.

JULY 25
National Merry-Go-Round Day

What do you call a carousel without brakes?

A merry-go-round-and-round-and-round . . .

What did the horse say when the carousel ride was over?

"Whoa!"

Where do unicorns ride the merry-go-round?

At a unicorn-ival

What do you do if you're surrounded by four polar bears, two lions, one tiger, and three bull elephants?

Stop the merry-go-round and get off.

JULY 26
National Aunts and Uncles Day

Who is married to Antarctica?

Uncle Arctica

What did the monkey say when he found out his sister had a baby?

"Well, I'll be a monkey's uncle!"

JULY 27
Bagpipe Appreciation Day

Why do bagpipers march when they play?

To get away from the noise.

194

JULY 28
National Soccer Day

What is a ghost's favorite position in soccer?

Ghoul-keeper

Why is Cinderella bad at soccer?

Because she runs away from the ball.

What are soccer players' favorite birds?

Pair-a-cleats

Why do soccer players do so well in school?

They use their heads.

Why do soccer players like spicy food?

Because it has a kick to it.

JULY 29
Global Tiger Day

When is water like a tiger?

When it springs from the ground.

What is the fiercest flower in the garden?
A tiger lily

What did the umpire say to the tiger?

"Three stripes and you're out!"

Who went into the tiger's lair and came out alive?

The tiger

JULY 30
World Snorkeling Day

Where can you go snorkeling in space?

In the gravi-sea

What does a snorkeler do when her lunch comes?

Dives right in!

JULY 31
National Mutt Day

How do dogs like to travel?

By mutt-a-cycle

What do dogs put on their pizza?

Mutts-arella

What do you call a dog who helps you carry hot things?

An oven mutt

MORE
JULY LAUGHS

Knock, knock.

Who's there?

July.

July who?

July awake at night counting sheep?

How do pandas stay cool in July?

They use bear conditioning.

Why did the robot go on summer vacation?

To recharge his batteries

Knock, knock.

Who's there?

Summer.

Summer who?

Summer these jokes are funny, but some aren't!

Where do sheep go on vacation?
To the baa-*hamas*

AUGUST

AUGUST 1
Spider-Man Day

What did Iron Man say to Spider-Man?

"Don't bug me."

What do you get when you cross Spider-Man with flatbread?

Pita Parker

What did Spider-Man do when he got a new car?

He took it out for a spin.

AUGUST 2
National Coloring Book Day

Why did the boy bring his coloring book to the zoo?

Because his art teacher told him to color between the lions.

Where do crayons go on vacation?

Colorado

What color is rain?

Watercolor

AUGUST 3
National Watermelon Day

When does red mean go and green mean stop?

When you are eating watermelon.

What do you get when you cross a watermelon with a school bus?

A fruit that can seat forty-five people

Why did the cantaloupe jump into the sea?

It wanted to become a watermelon.

AUGUST 4
International Owl Awareness Day

What do you call an owl magician?

Whoo-*dini*

> ### What is an owl's favorite soft drink?
> Hoot *beer*

What subject do owls like to study?

Owl-*gebra*

What is an owl's favorite kind of pepper?

Owl-*apeño*

AUGUST 5
National Oyster Day

What is an oyster's strongest friend?

A mussel

What kind of car does an oyster drive?

A clam-borghini

What kind of picture does an oyster take?

A shell-fie

AUGUST 6
National Root Beer Float Day

How do you make a hippopotamus float?

With two scoops of ice cream, a bottle of root beer, and a hippopotamus

---

AUGUST 7
National Lighthouse Day

What building is easy to lift?

A lighthouse

How do lighthouse keepers communicate?
With shine language

AUGUST 8
International Cat Day

Why are cats good at video games?

They all have nine lives.

Where do you find a Christmas present for a cat?

In a catalog

Why did the cat lie on the computer?

To keep an eye on the mouse

National Book Lovers' Day

Where are you when you fall asleep reading a book?

Under the covers

Why was the mummy afraid to go to the library?

Because his books were thousands of years overdue.

Which kind of book is an oilcan's favorite?

Non-friction

What do planets like to read?

Comet books

AUGUST 10
National Lazy Day

Which bug never does its chores?

A lazy-bug

What do you call a lazy baby kangaroo?

A pouch potato

What do lazy dogs do?

They chase parked cars.

What did the lazy cat say to the rat?

"Catch you later."

What do you call a lazy butcher?

A meat loafer

AUGUST 11
National Play in the Sand Day

What do crabs use to clean their claws?

Sand-itizer

What do you call a witch who likes the beach but is scared of the water?

A chicken sand-witch

Knock, knock.

Who's there?

Sandal.

Sandal who?

Sandal sticks to your legs if you get it wet.

AUGUST 12
World Elephant Day

What has wheels and a trunk, but no engine?

An elephant on roller skates

What do elephants wear on their legs?

Ele-pants

How can you tell when an elephant is in the refrigerator?

You can't shut the door.

What is beautiful, gray, and wears glass slippers?

Cinder-elephant

AUGUST 13
International Left-Handers Day

What did the left hand say to the other hand?

"How does it feel to always be right?"

What can you hold in your left hand that you can't hold in your right hand?

Your right elbow

Cameron: How do you like your new gloves?

Carrie: They're both left-handed! On the one hand it's great, on the other hand it just isn't right.

World Lizard Day

What powerful reptile can you find in the Emerald City?

The Lizard of Oz

Why do geckos stay inside during winter weather?

They don't like b-lizards.

What do you call a rich lizard?

A chameleon-aire

AUGUST 15
National Relaxation Day

Why don't mummies like to take vacations?

They're afraid to relax and unwind.

Where do geologists like to relax?

In a rocking chair

National Roller Coaster Day

How does it sound when you sneeze on a roller coaster?

Ah-ah-ah-ah-ah-ah-ah-ah-choo!

Why did the goose go on the roller coaster?

To show it was no chicken

What is an Arctic bear's favorite ride at the amusement park?

The polar coaster

AUGUST 17
National I Love My Feet Day

What did the feet say when they were having fun?

"This is toe-rrific!"

What color socks do pandas wear?

They don't wear socks. They have bear feet!

AUGUST 18
National Fajita Day

Knock, knock.

Who's there?

Fajita.

Fajita who?

Fajita another fajita, I'll be stuffed!

AUGUST 19
National Potato Day

What's the difference between a potato and an onion?

No one cries when you cut up a potato.

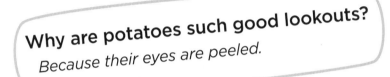

Why are potatoes such good lookouts?
Because their eyes are peeled.

What do you call a spinning potato?

A rotate-o

What do you get when it rains potatoes?

Spud-dles

Why did the potato cross the road?

It saw a fork up ahead.

AUGUST 20
World Mosquito Day

How did the mosquito become an actor?

It passed its screen test.

What is the worst place for a mosquito?

A room full of clapping people

AUGUST 21
Poet's Day

How do poets say hello?

"Hey, haven't we metaphor?"

What did the poet say to Luke Skywalker?

Metaphors be with you.

AUGUST 22
National Eat a Peach Day

Visitor: You sure grow a lot of peaches around here. What do you do with all of them?

Farmer: We eat what we can and can what we can't.

AUGUST 23
National Sponge Cake Day

What's the best thing to eat in a bathtub?

A sponge cake

Sasha: Here, Dad, try some of my sponge cake.

Dad: Hmmm . . . it's a bit tough.

Sasha: I don't understand. I used a really fresh sponge.

Vesuvius Day

What does Mount Vesuvius eat for dinner?

Lava-cados

What did the angry volcano say to the other volcano?

"Stop int-erupt-ing me!"

What is a volcano?

A mountain with hiccups

What is Mount Vesuvius's favorite food?

Magma-roni and cheese

AUGUST 25
National Banana Split Day

Why was the apple lonely?

Because the banana split!

Where do you learn to make a banana split?

In sundae school

What is ice cream's favorite gymnastic move?

The banana split

AUGUST 26
National Dog Day

What do you call a dog who builds doghouses?

A bark-itect

What is a dog's favorite kind of candy?

Pupper-mints

Why was the dog so good in school?

He was the teacher's pet.

What dog loves to take bubble baths?
A sham-poodle

When is a dog's tail like a farmer's cart?

When it's a-waggin'

National Banana Lovers' Day

Why don't bananas snore?

Because they don't want to wake the rest of the bunch.

How do monkeys get downstairs?

They slide down the banana-ster.

What is the best time to eat a banana?

When the moment is ripe.

> **What is yellow and writes?**
> *A ballpoint banana*

AUGUST 28
National Cherry Turnover Day

Why did the jelly roll?

Because it saw the cherry turnover.

AUGUST 29
National Lemon Juice Day

Knock, knock.

Who's there?

Lemon juice.

Lemon juice who?

Lemon juice you to my friend.

AUGUST 30
Frankenstein Day

How did newspapers describe the day Frankenstein's monster was created?

"Shocking!"

Why did Frankenstein's monster like the stand-up comic?

Because she kept him in stitches.

What did the critics say about Frankenstein's piece of art?

"What a monster-piece!"

- -

AUGUST 31
National Trail Mix Day

What is a train's favorite snack?

Rail mix

MORE
AUGUST LAUGHS

Knock, knock.

Who's there?

August.

August who?

August of wind almost blew me away!

What's a math teacher's favorite season?

Summer

What did the baker do over summer vacation?

He loafed around.

How do sheep celebrate the end of summer?

They have a baa-baa-*cue*

What do you call a labrador on the beach in August?

A hot dog

SEPTEMBER

SEPTEMBER 1
National Sushi Day

What do you call sushi that's on sale?

A raw deal

> **How old was Yuki when he first had sushi?**
> *Tuna half*

What did the sushi say to the rice ball?

"Let's chopstick together."

How did the family like the sushi restaurant?

They were soy happy.

SEPTEMBER 2
World Coconut Day

What is hairy and coughs?

A coconut with a cold

Mom: If I had five coconuts and I gave you three, how many would I have left?

Nia: I don't know.

Mom: Why not?

Nia: In our school we do arithmetic with apples and oranges.

SEPTEMBER 3
U.S. Bowling League Day

Why do tires get upset when they go bowling?

Because they never make strikes, just spares.

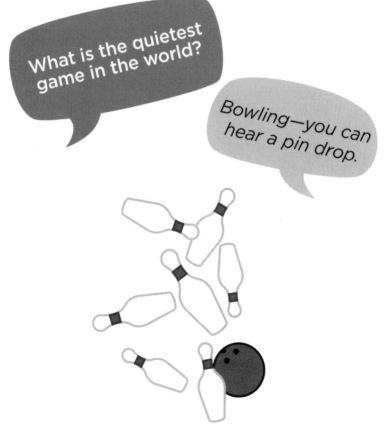

What is the quietest game in the world?

Bowling—you can hear a pin drop.

SEPTEMBER 4
National Newspaper Carrier Day

What newspaper did the cave dwellers read?

The Prehistoric Times

What newspaper do cows read?

The Daily Moos

Why does the electric eel read the newspaper?

To keep up on current events.

SEPTEMBER 5
National Be Late for Something Day

What kind of candy is always late for class?

Chocolate

Why were *U, V, W, X, Y,* and *Z* late to the tea party?

Because they always come after T.

Why was the broom late for school?

It over-swept.

National Read a Book Day

What color are all the books you've finished?

Red

What kind of books do mountain climbers like to read?

Cliff-hangers

What do cows read to their babies at bedtime?

Dairy tales

Knock, knock.

Who's there?

Rita.

Rita who?

Rita book. It's fun!

SEPTEMBER 7
National Salami Day

What did the ham do when he wanted to talk to the salami?

He called a meat-ing.

What kind of cold cuts do opera singers like to eat?

So-la-mi

SEPTEMBER 8
National Iguana Awareness Day

Knock, knock.

Who's there?

Iguana.

Iguana who?

Iguana hold your hand.

SEPTEMBER 9
National Teddy Bear Day

Why can't you feed a teddy bear?

Because it's already stuffed.

- -

SEPTEMBER 10
Sew Be It Day

Who makes a tutu for a _Brontosaurus_?

A dino-sewer

How much does it hurt to sit on an embroidery needle?

Sew much!

> **Why do porcupines love to sew?**
>
> *They never run out of needles.*

Customer: How's business?
Tailor: Sew-sew.

SEPTEMBER 11
National Make Your Bed Day

Mom: Dan, did you make your bed today?

Dan: Yes, Mom, but I think it would be better to buy one.

SEPTEMBER 12
National Chocolate Milkshake Day

How do you make a chocolate milkshake?

Give it a good scare.

International Chocolate Day

What is a sheep's favorite candy?

A chocolate baaa-*r*

What did the happy chocolate say to the cranky chocolate?

"Don't have a meltdown."

Knock, knock.

Who's there?

Candy.

Candy who?

Candy boy have another piece of chocolate?

National Cream-Filled Doughnut Day

How can you tell when a vampire has been in a bakery?

All the cream has been sucked out of the cream-filled doughnuts.

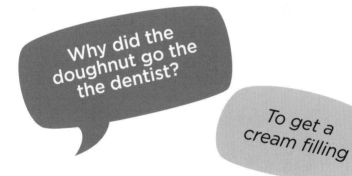

Why did the doughnut go the the dentist?

To get a cream filling

Doctor: How are you feeling?

Doughnut: Well, kind of empty.

Doctor: Hmm, that's unusual. You're a Boston cream!

SEPTEMBER 15
Make a Hat Day

What do you call a hat that you wear on your knee?

A kneecap

Why can't you take a picture of a tiger with a hat?

Because you can't take a picture with a hat.

SEPTEMBER 16
National Guacamole Day

Why did the paparazzi follow the avocado?

He was a guac star.

How does a robot eat guacamole?

With computer chips

SEPTEMBER 17
International Country Music Day

How many country musicians does it take to change a light bulb?

Five. One to change the bulb, and four to sing about how much they'll miss the old one.

What do long-distance truckers listen to?

Cross-country music

Is the song "Africa" by Toto country music?

No, it's continent music.

SEPTEMBER 18
National Cheeseburger Day

Knock, knock.

Who's there?

Wendy Waiter.

Wendy Waiter who?

Wendy Waiter gets here, order me a cheeseburger.

SEPTEMBER 19
International Talk Like a Pirate Day

What kind of socks does a pirate wear?

Arrr-gyle

What did the pirate say on his eightieth birthday?

Aye, matey!

How much does a pirate pay to get his ears pierced?

A buccaneer

Why does it take pirates so long to learn the alphabet?

Because they spend years at C.

National Pepperoni Pizza Day

What did the pepperoni say when it needed to take notes?

"May I have a pizza paper and a pen?"

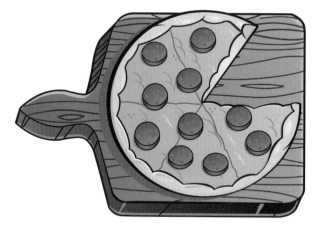

What is a dog's favorite topping on a pizza?

Pup-peroni

What kind of pizza makes people sneeze?

Pepper-only pizza

Miniature Golf Day

What is an elf's favorite sport?

Miniature golf

Why are old socks good for mini golf?
Because they have plenty of holes.

Where do mini golfers go after a game?

A tee party

What did the astronaut get when he went mini-golfing?
A black hole in one

SEPTEMBER 22
National Ice-Cream Cone Day

Why did the ice-cream cone read the newspaper?

To get the latest scoop

How do unicorns eat their ice cream?

In a uni-cone

What did the ice cream say when it was cold?

"I'm chilled to the cone!"

SEPTEMBER 23
National Great American Potpie Day

Diner: Waiter, there's no chicken in my chicken potpie!

Waiter: Would you expect to find a dog in a dog biscuit, sir?

What do you get if you cross a train with a potpie?

Puff pastry

SEPTEMBER 24
National Punctuation Day

What is the world's longest punctuation mark?

The hundred-yard dash

What's the difference between a cat and a comma?

A cat has claws at the end of its paws, but a comma is a pause at the end of a clause.

What type of websites have the best grammar?

Any URL ending with .comma

Natalie: Hey, look! What are they doing at that punctuation party?

Ben: I don't know, but they're hyphen fun!

SEPTEMBER 25
National Lobster Day

Why does the ocean roar?

You would, too, if you had lobsters in your bed.

Why don't lobsters share?

They're shellfish.

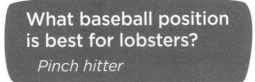

What baseball position is best for lobsters?

Pinch hitter

What did the lobster give to the teacher?

A crab apple

SEPTEMBER 26
National Lumberjack Day

What is a lumberjack's favorite month?

Sep-TIMBER!

What's the difference between a bunny and a lumberjack?

One chews and hops, and the other hews and chops.

> ### Where does a lumberjack go to buy things?
> *The chopping center*

What kind of clinic would a lumberjack visit for a toothache?

An axe-i-dental clinic

SEPTEMBER 27
National Scarf Day

What did the scarf say to the hat?

*"I'll hang around.
You go on ahead."*

What is a dog's favorite winter accessory?

A sc-arf!

SEPTEMBER 28
National Good Neighbor Day

Why did the stallion cross the road?

To meet his new neigh-*bors*

SEPTEMBER 29
World Heart Day

How does a heart play music?

It follows the beat.

Why did the vampire become a vegetarian?

He heard steak was bad for his heart.

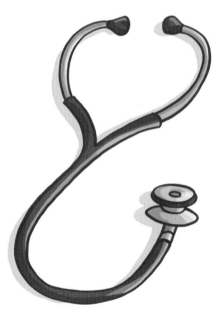

SEPTEMBER 30
National Chewing Gum Day

What kind of gum do scientists chew?

Ex-spearmint gum

Why did the chewing gum cross the road?

Because it was stuck to the chicken's foot.

What kind of fish likes bubble gum?

A blowfish

What do you get if you cross a railroad engine with a stick of gum?

A chew-chew train

MORE
SEPTEMBER LAUGHS

How far is it from September to December?

Just a short fall.

Why do birds fly south for the winter?

Because it's too far to walk.

Knock, knock.

Who's there?

Noah.

Noah who?

Noah more summer—it's time for school!

> **Why do trees hate going to school in the fall?**
> *Because they're easily stumped.*

Which month has a sore throat?

Strep-tember

What did the tree say to autumn?

"Leaf me alone."

OCTOBER 1
National Hair Day

How does the man in the moon cut his hair?

Eclipse it

What is a hot dog's favorite hairstyle?

A bun

Why do bees have sticky hair?

Because they use honeycombs.

Where do sheep go to get their hair cut?

To the baa-baa-*shop*

OCTOBER 2
National Name Your Car Day

What kind of car has whiskers and purrs?

A Cat-illac

Which kind of car lives at a ranch?

A Mustang

What kind of cars do dogs drive?

Hound-as

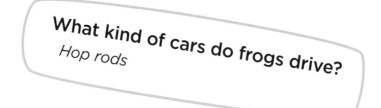

What kind of cars do frogs drive?
Hop rods

OCTOBER 3
National Butterfly and Hummingbird Day

Why couldn't the butterfly go to the dance?

Because it was a moth ball.

Where do butterflies sleep?

On cater-pillows

Why do hummingbirds hum?

Because they don't know the words.

OCTOBER 4
World Animal Day

Which animals are the coldest?

Mice, because they're three-fourths ice.

What animals can jump higher than a house?

All of them. Houses can't jump.

What do you get when you cross a sheep and a porcupine?

An animal that can knit its own sweaters.

What is a vampire's favorite animal?

A giraffe

Knock, knock.

Who's there?

Owl.

Owl who?

I'm owl out of animal jokes.

OCTOBER 5
World Teachers' Day

What do you do if a teacher rolls her eyes at you?

Pick them up and roll them back to her.

What's a teacher's favorite nation?

Explanation

What do you say when comforting a grammar teacher?

"There, their, they're."

What do you call a teacher who never says your name right?

Ms. Pronounce

OCTOBER 6
National Noodle Day

Why is ramen the smartest food?

It always uses its noodle.

What's long, skinny, and beats on a drum?

Yankee Noodle

- -

OCTOBER 7
National Bathtub Day

What bird steals soap from the bathtub?

A robber duck

Knock, knock.

Who's there?

Dwayne.

Dwayne who?

Dwayne the bathtub before it overflows!

OCTOBER 8
World Octopus Day

What can make an octopus laugh?

Ten tickles

Why did the octopus beat the shark in a fight?

Because the octopus was well armed.

What lives in the sea and carries a lot of people?

An octo-bus

OCTOBER 9
World Post Day

What did the envelope say to the stamp?

"Stick with me, and we'll go places."

When is a mailbox like the alphabet?

When it's full of letters.

What do you call it when everyone runs to the post office at the same time?

A stampede

OCTOBER 10
National Cake Decorating Day

Why do hockey players make the best birthday cakes?

Because they know all about icing.

Why is it better to eat cakes in the rain?

You get more sprinkles.

What is the last thing a snowman does when he bakes a cake?

He frosts it.

What position do cakes play in baseball?

The batter.

OCTOBER 11
National Spread Joy Day

Why did the dog leap for joy?

Joy was holding the cookies.

- -

OCTOBER 12
National Farmer's Day

Why did the farmer cross the road?

To bring back his chicken

What did the apple tree say to the farmer?

"Quit picking on me."

What is the definition of a farmer?

Someone who is outstanding in his field.

OCTOBER 13
National Train Your Brain Day

Annette: Guess what I've had stuck in my head for a long time?

Abby: I don't know. What?

Annette: My brain!

What do you call a really smart doe?

A brain-deer

Which organ is the only one that named itself?

The brain

Why did the zombie do so well on his exam?

Because it was a no-brainer.

OCTOBER 14
National Dessert Day

What is a statue's favorite dessert?

Marble cake

What does glue have for dessert?

A paste-ry

What is a turkey's favorite dessert?

Cherry gobbler

Why did the moon say no to dessert?

Because it was full.

OCTOBER 15
National Mushroom Day

How would you know if you had too many toadstools in your trash can?

There wouldn't be mushroom inside.

What is a mushroom's favorite vacation spot?

Portabella

Why was the mushroom a big hit at the party?

He was a fungi.

OCTOBER 16
Dictionary Day

If you find a rabbit eating your dictionary, what should you do?

Take the words right out of its mouth.

Where can you always find happiness?

In the dictionary

What does an expensive TV have in common with a dictionary on top of a mountain?

They're both high definition.

OCTOBER 17
National Pasta Day

What do you call a fake noodle?

An im-pasta

What did the macaroni say as it left the cafeteria?

"Pasta la vista!"

What is a tortoise's favorite pasta?

Turtle-ini

What pasta do dogs like?

Fetch-uccini

OCTOBER 18
National Mashed Potato Day

What do you get when you cross potato plants with squash plants?

Mashed potatoes

Knock, knock.

Who's there?

Pastor.

Pastor who?

Pastor mashed potatoes, please.

- -

OCTOBER 19
National Kentucky Day

Knock, knock.

Who's there?

Kentucky.

Kentucky who?

Dad Kentucky you in at night.

OCTOBER 20
International Chefs Day

What do you call a turtle chef?

A slow cooker

Why did the chef double-check the ingredients before making a quesadilla?

In quesadilla there was a problem.

- - - - - - - - - - - - - - - - - - - -

OCTOBER 21
International Day of the Nacho

Knock, knock.

Who's there?

Nacho cheese.

Nacho cheese who?

That is nacho cheese, so give it back!

OCTOBER 22
National Nut Day

What did the nut say when it sneezed?

"Cashew!"

What is a robot's favorite party snack?

Mixed nuts

How do you catch an elephant?

Hide in a bush and make a noise like a peanut.

Knock, knock.

Who's there?

Cash.

Cash who?

No thank you, I prefer peanuts.

OCTOBER 23
National Croc Day

What kind of shoes is Captain Hook afraid of?

Crocs

OCTOBER 24
National Bologna Day

Why shouldn't you trust a sandwich?

Because it may be full of baloney.

What is the opposite of bologna?

Above knee

OCTOBER 25
International Artist Day

Why could the artist cross the bridge whenever he wanted to?

Because it was a drawbridge.

> ### What do alien artists paint?
> *Mars-terpieces*

What did the artist say to the wall?

"One more crack like that and I'll plaster you."

OCTOBER 26
National Pumpkin Day

Who is the leader of all jack-o'-lanterns?

The Pump-king

Why was Cinderella such a bad figure skater?

Her coach was a pumpkin.

What did the orange pumpkin say to the green pumpkin?

"Why orange you orange?"

Who helps little pumpkins cross the road safely?

The crossing gourd

What do you call a pumpkin that thinks it's a comedian?

A joke-o'-lantern

OCTOBER 27
National Black Cat Day

When is it bad luck to see a black cat?

When you're a mouse.

OCTOBER 28
World Lemur Day

Why did the lemur cross the road?

He had to take care of some monkey business.

What do lemurs drive?

Madagas-cars

National Oatmeal Day

Why was the oatmeal sad?

No raisin

What do ships eat for breakfast?

Boat-meal

OCTOBER 30
National Candy Corn Day

What treat do eye doctors give out on Halloween?

Candy corneas

What crop does a farmer with a sweet tooth grow?

Candy corn

What do you get if you cross a candy corn and a werewolf?

A corn dog

Halloween

What does Dracula drink on Halloween?

De-coffin-ated coffee

What does an elephant say on Halloween?

"Trunk-or-treat!"

Why did the police officer ticket the ghost on Halloween?

It didn't have a haunting license.

Why don't ghosts like rain on Halloween?

It dampens their spirits.

Why do mummies love Halloween?

Because of all the free candy wrappers.

MORE
OCTOBER LAUGHS

Knock, knock.

Who's there?

Omar.

Omar who?

Omar gosh, it's October already!

Which month is always on time?

Clock-tober

> **What did one leaf say to the other leaf?**
>
> *"I'm falling for you!"*

Which season is the cutest?

Awww-*tumn*

A book never written:
Favorite Fall Flowers
by Chris-Ann T. Mums

NOVEMBER

NOVEMBER 1
National Brush Day

What do astronauts use to brush their teeth?

Tooth-space

What does a musician brush his teeth with?

A tuba toothpaste

What happened to the sheep that forgot to brush its teeth?

It got baaa-d breath

Why do vampires brush their teeth?

To prevent bat breath.

Henry: Mom, I can't.

Mom: Henry, never say you can't do something.

Henry: OK. Then will you please help me put the toothpaste back in the tube?

NOVEMBER 2
Día de los Muertos (Day of the Dead)

What are the best jokes for Day of the Dead?

Humerus ones

What did the papel picado say to the string?

"Let's hang out together!"

NOVEMBER 3
World Jellyfish Day

What do whales eat on picnics?

Peanut blubber and jellyfish sandwiches

What seafood goes well with peanut butter?

Jellyfish

What do you put on a sting from a jellyfish?

Peanut butter

National Candy Day

What is a rabbit's favorite candy?

Lolli-hops

What do you call a house full of candy?

Dessert-ed

What has teeth but can't eat candy?

A comb

What is a playground's favorite candy?

Recess pieces

NOVEMBER 5
American Football Day

What do championship football players eat their cereal in?

Super bowls

> **Why did the football coach send in his second string?**
> *To tie up the game*

What kind of bees are bad at football?

Fumble-bees

Why did the football coach go to the bank?

He wanted his quarterback.

NOVEMBER 6
National Saxophone Day

Why did the bear put his saxophone in the freezer?

To make cool music

Why are saxophone players so smart?
They reed a lot.

Why did the musician leave the concert?

He needed to put on a fresh pair of sax.

National Bittersweet Chocolate with Almonds Day

Knock, knock.

Who's there?

Almond.

Almond who?

Almond the other side of the door.

What do you call an almond in outer space?

An astro-nut

Where can you go to learn about almonds?

The inter-nut.

NOVEMBER 8
National
X-ray Day

Ray: What is before *Y* and after *W*?

Bill: *X*, Ray.

Ray: I never knew that X-ray was a letter of the alphabet.

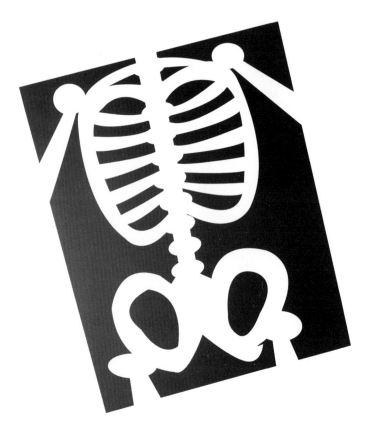

NOVEMBER 9
Go to an Art Museum Day

Knock, knock.

Who's there?

Mozart.

Mozart who?

Mozart is found in museums.

NOVEMBER 10
The Marine Corps Birthday

If sailors and marines were playing basketball and all of the marines fouled out, who would they send in next?

The submarines

NOVEMBER 11
National Sundae Day

What's black and white and red all over?

A chocolate sundae with ketchup on top

What do you call an ice-cream truck operator?

A sundae driver

What does ice cream wear to church?

Its sundae best

NOVEMBER 12
National Fancy Rat and Mouse Day

Why didn't the fancy rat take a bath?

Because he was already squeaky clean.

What kind of party do fancy mice throw when they move into a new home?

A mouse-warming party

NOVEMBER 13
National Hug a Musician Day

What did the musicians name their daughter?

Melody

What did the musician say when he had to leave the rehearsal for a few minutes?

"I'll be right Bach."

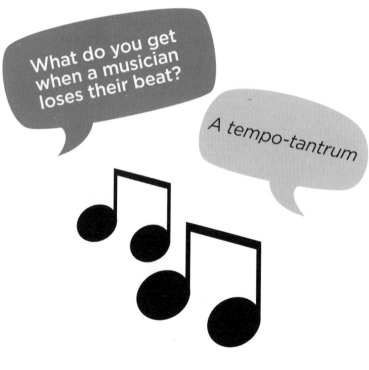

NOVEMBER 14
National Pickle Day

Knock, knock.

Who's there?

Pickle.

Pickle who?

Pickle little flower for your mother.

Why did the pickle go to the school nurse's office?

He felt dill.

Which instrument plays only sour notes?

The pickle-o

What's black, white, black, white, black, white, and green?

Three skunks arguing over a pickle

NOVEMBER 15
National Drumming Day

What's the absolute best present?

*A broken drum—
you can't beat it!*

How many drummers does it take to change a light bulb?

One, two . . . one, two, three, four!

What can turkeys use to play an instrument?

Drumsticks

NOVEMBER 16
National Button Day

What did the button say to the tailor?

"Give me a hand. I'm hanging on by a thread!"

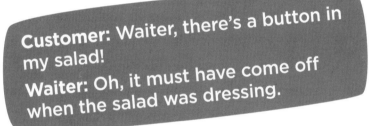

Customer: Waiter, there's a button in my salad!

Waiter: Oh, it must have come off when the salad was dressing.

Teacher: Freddy, give me a sentence using the word *fascinate*.

Freddy: I have nine buttons on my jacket, but I can only fasten eight.

NOVEMBER 17
National Hiking Day

How do fleas travel?

They itch-hike.

What should you take on a hike in the desert?

A thirst aid kit

Where's the best place to eat while hiking?

A fork in the road

NOVEMBER 18
National Princess Day

What is it called when a princess gets a sore throat?

A royal pain in the neck

What do you call a princess's horse?

Her maje-steed

NOVEMBER 19
National Play Monopoly Day

Which animal would you never want to play Monopoly with?

A cheetah

What's an astronaut's favorite board game?

Moon-opoly

NOVEMBER 20
National Child's Day

What did the buffalo say to his child when he left on a trip?

"Bison."

What did the snake give to his child at bedtime?

A goodnight hiss

The parents have seven daughters. Each daughter has one brother. How many children do the parents have total?

Eight children. There's only one brother!

NOVEMBER 21
World Television Day

What's the difference between a television and a newspaper?

Ever try swatting a fly with a television?

Teacher: Where is the English Channel?

Reid: I don't know. My TV doesn't pick it up!

What is a squirrel's favorite way to watch TV?

Nut-flix

> **Why wouldn't the fish watch TV?**
> *He was afraid he'd get hooked.*

NOVEMBER 22
Go for a Ride Day

What do you say to a tree frog who needs a ride?

"Hop in!"

What does a snail riding on a turtle's back say?

"Woo-hoo!"

- -

NOVEMBER 23
National Eat a Cranberry Day

What's small, round, and blue?

A cranberry holding its breath

Why did the farmer plant cranberries on the road?

He wanted cranberry juice.

Celebrate Your Unique Talent Day

What do you call a hawk that can draw and play the guitar at the same time?

Talon-ted

What did the fox do for the talent show?

The foxtrot

How did the sledgehammer do in the talent show?

She was a smashing success.

NOVEMBER 25
National Play Day with Dad

Jessie: Can you take me to the park on Friday?

Dad: Sure, but if it rains on Friday, what will we do?

Jessie: Go the day before.

Jordan: Will you teach me how to catch a fish?

Dad: Sure, son! It's easy. I'll just toss this trout to you.

Why do dads take an extra pair of socks when they go golfing?

In case they get a hole in one!

NOVEMBER 26
National Cake Day

What kind of cake do you get after a big meal?

A stomach-cake

How do cats bake honey cake?
From scratch

Knock, knock.

Who's there?

Samoa.

Samoa who?

Samoa cake, please!

NOVEMBER 27
National Bavarian Cream Pie Day

What's the best thing to put in a Bavarian cream pie?

Your teeth

NOVEMBER 28
Red Planet Day

How did Mary's little lamb get to Mars?

By rocket sheep

What's the Red Planet's favorite song?

"Mars and Stripes Forever"

What is soft and white and comes from Mars?

Martian-mallows

What do you get when you cross a kangaroo and an alien?

A Mars-upial

What do Martians who use the metric system say when they land on Earth?

"Take me to your liter."

National Square Dancing Day

What kind of dancing gets you in shape?

Square dancing

What do you do at a geometry party?

A square dance

National Mississippi Day

Why does Mississippi have the best vision out of all the states?

Because it has four i's.

Who is Mr. Sippi's wife?

Mississippi

MORE
NOVEMBER LAUGHS

What's a fire's least favorite month?

No-ember

What always comes at the end of November?

The letter R

Why are trees so easygoing?

Because, every autumn, they let loose.

When winter arrives, what happens?

Autumn leaves

DECEMBER

DECEMBER 1
National Christmas Lights Day

Why did the dinosaur eat the Christmas lights?

Because he wanted a light snack.

Where is a cat when the Christmas lights go out?

In the dark

What happened to the dog when he swallowed a strand of Christmas lights?

He barked with delight.

DECEMBER 2
Play Basketball Day

What do you do if the basketball court gets flooded?

Call in the subs

> ### Why do basketball players love doughnuts?
> *Because they can dunk them.*

Why shouldn't you have ducks on your basketball team?

They always make fowl shots.

What is a basketball player's favorite cheese?
Swish

DECEMBER 3
National Make a Gift Day

What is an elf's favorite music?

Gift rap

After the first two Wise Men presented their gifts of gold and frankincense, what did the third one say?

"Wait! There's myrrh!"

Why does Santa take presents to children around the world?

Because the presents won't take themselves!

Corey: I made these socks for my brother at college.

Mikayla: That's a great holiday gift, but why did you knit three socks?

Corey: In his last letter, he said he'd grown another foot!

DECEMBER 4
International Cheetah Day

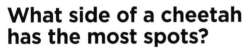

What side of a cheetah has the most spots?

The outside

> **What do cheetahs like to eat?**
> *Fast food*

Why don't cheetahs ever take baths?

Because they don't want to be spotless.

- -

DECEMBER 5
International Ninja Day

Who was the most dangerous cookie?

The ninja-bread man

What is a ninja's favorite drink?
Punch

DECEMBER 6
Mitten Tree Day

Knock, knock.

Who's there?

Hansel.

Hansel who?

Hansel freeze out here if you don't wear your mittens.

> **What happened when the cat ate a ball of yarn?**
>
> *She had mittens.*

DECEMBER 7
National Letter Writing Day

How does a hog write a letter?

With a pigpen

DECEMBER 8
Pretend to Be a Time Traveler Day

Bob: Want to hear a joke about time travel?

Joe: Sure.

Bob: Actually, never mind. You didn't like it.

DECEMBER 9
National Llama Day

What do alpacas sing at Christmas time?

"Fa-la-la-la-laaa, la-la-llama!"

What do llamas get when they graduate high school?

A dip-llama

What is a llama's favorite drink?

Llama-nade

DECEMBER 10
Nobel Prize Day

Why didn't the scientist have a doorbell?

He wanted to win the No-bell Prize.

DECEMBER 11
International Mountain Day

Why shouldn't you play hide-and-seek with a mountain?

It peaks!

Which mountain is the sleepiest?

Mount Ever-rest

Before Mount Everest was discovered, what was the highest mountain in the world?

Mount Everest— it just wasn't discovered yet.

DECEMBER 12
National Gingerbread House Day

Why was the gingerbread house robbed?

Because of its dough.

Where do gingerbread people sleep?

Under cookie sheets

National Hot Cocoa Day

What do you call someone who's crazy about hot chocolate?

A cocoa-nut

Why did the elephant stand on the marshmallow?

Because he didn't want to fall into the hot cocoa.

Knock, knock.

Who's there?

Stirrup.

Stirrup who?

Stirrup some hot chocolate for me, please.

DECEMBER 14
International Monkey Day

What do you call a monkey with all his bananas taken away?

Furious George

What is the first thing a monkey learns in school?

His Ape, B, C's.

What does a monkey use to cover a scratch?

A banana-dage

What is a monkey's favorite dessert?

Meringue-utan

DECEMBER 15
International Tea Day

What do you ask a thirsty tyrannosaur?

"Tea, Rex?"

Knock, knock.

Who's there?

Alec.

Alec who?

Alec tea, but I don't like coffee.

Why did dinosaurs drink cold tea?
Because fire wasn't discovered yet.

What did they wear at the Boston Tea Party?

T-shirts

DECEMBER 16
National Chocolate-Covered Anything Day

What do you get when you dip a little feline in chocolate?

A Kitty Kat bar

What do you call a monkey covered in chocolate?

A chocolate chimp

DECEMBER 17
Wright Brothers Day

Two wrongs don't make a right, but what do two rights make?

Two Wrights make an airplane.

DECEMBER 18
Flake Appreciation Day

What's white and goes up?

A confused snowflake.

What did one snowflake say to the other?

You're one of a kind.

Knock, knock.

Who's there?

Snow.

Snow who?

Snow way today won't be a snow day.

Why did the boy only wear one snow boot?

There was only a 50 percent chance of snow.

DECEMBER 19
Look for an Evergreen Day

Why do Christmas trees recycle?

They are evergreen.

How do evergreen trees like their ice cream served?

In a pine cone

Go Caroling Day

What is a tiger's favorite Christmas carol?

"Jungle Bells"

What do you call an insect who loves Christmas carols?

A humbug

What has forty feet and sings?

Twenty Christmas carolers

How can you tell carolers are coming to your house?

They jingle all the way.

What carol is heard in the desert?

"Camel Ye Faithful"

DECEMBER 21
National Maine Day

What did the state say when it got only one question wrong on the test?

"Oh, Maine!"

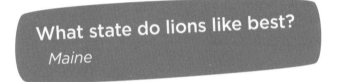

What state do lions like best?

Maine

Who helps deliver Christmas gifts to New England?

Maine-deer

DECEMBER 22
National Cookie Exchange Day

What kind of cookies do sea serpents like to eat?

Chocolate ship

What is slime's favorite dessert?

Sticker-doodle cookies

Allyah: I have a super-secret cookie recipe.

Yoni: What is it?

Allyah: I can't tell you. It's on a knead-to-dough basis.

National Christmas Movie Marathon Day

What is a chipmunk's favorite Christmas movie?

The Nutcracker

What is a shark's favorite Christmas movie?

Santa Jaws Is Coming to Town

What is a baker's favorite holiday movie?

A Charlie Brownie Christmas

What Christmas movie do Santa's helpers love most?

Elf, *of course.*

What is a dentist's favorite Christmas movie?

The Molar Express

DECEMBER 24
Christmas Eve

Why does Santa go down the chimney on Christmas Eve?

Because it soots him.

What should you do if your car breaks down on Christmas Eve?

Get a mistle-tow.

DECEMBER 25
Christmas Day

How does Rudolph know when Christmas is coming?

He refers to his calen-deer.

What did one cow say to the other cow on Christmas Day?

"Dairy Christmas!"

What does everyone start Christmas Day with?

The letter C

How did Sofia greet her father on Christmas morning?

"Feliz Navi-Dad!"

How do you tell the weather on Christmas morning?

Look out the window.

DECEMBER 26
Kwanzaa

Knock, knock.

Who's there?

Mayor.

Mayor who?

Mayor Kwanzaa be filled with peace and unity!

DECEMBER 27
Make Cutout Snowflakes Day

Where does a snowflake go to dance?

A snowball!

What is a snowman's favorite cereal?

Frosted Snowflakes

National Card Playing Day

What has thirteen hearts but no other organs?

A deck of playing cards.

> **Why couldn't the sailors play cards?**
>
> *The captain was standing on the deck.*

Two crayons were playing Uno. The first crayon said, "I have fifteen cards."

The second crayon said, "How did you get so many?"

"I had to draw," the first crayon replied.

DECEMBER 29
Ticktock Day

How can you tell that a clock is hungry?

It goes back four seconds.

> **What happened to the dog that swallowed a watch?**
>
> *It got ticks.*

Why did the clock go to the principal's office?

For tocking too much

Jack: What time is it?

Tim: I don't know.

Jack: Well, what does your watch say?

Tim: Ticktock, ticktock.

DECEMBER 30
National Bacon Day

Where does bacon go on vacation?

The Pig-cific Ocean

What did the sign outside the pig motel say?

No Bacon-cy

Why did the bacon laugh?

Because the egg told a funny yolk.

Sophia: Hey, Dad. There's no bacon left!
Dad: Sorry, I guess I hogged it all.

DECEMBER 31
New Year's Eve

What time is it when the clock strikes thirteen on New Year's Eve?

Time to fix the clock

Where is New Year's Eve very mathematical?

Times Square

Why did the boy put a slice of bread in the toaster at midnight on December 31?

He wanted to make a New Year's toast.

What did Adam say to his wife on December 31?

"It's New Year's Eve, Eve!"

MORE
DECEMBER LAUGHS

What did the snowflake say to the fallen leaf?

You're so last season.

Which moves faster in winter: heat or cold?

Heat! It's easy to catch cold.

What is the coldest month of the year?

Decem-brrrr

> ## What do you have in December that you don't have in any other month?
>
> *The letter* D

What wears a coat in the winter and pants in the summer?

A dog

Mel: I'd like to buy a winter coat.
Clerk: How long would you like it?
Mel: I'll probably need it all winter.

Which season is the most competitive?

Winter

Why did the snowplow driver enjoy her work?

Because there's no business like snow business.

FLOATING HOLIDAYS

Lunar New Year

What do dragons eat to celebrate Lunar New Year?

Firecrackers

What did one lantern say to the other?

"Why don't you lighten up?"

Dad: Why is there a journal by the dumplings?

Jae: In case they want to write about their fillings.

Holi

What is the Holi festival's loudest colored powder?

Yellow

Akash: I thought I got covered in Holi powder, but my clothes are clean!

Meera: It must have been a pigment of your imagination.

Knock, knock.

Who's there?

Hugh.

Hugh who?

Hues of colors are in the sky today!

What is a shirt's favorite holiday?
The Festival of Collars

What is a gujia's least favorite day?

Fry day.

Easter

How can you tell where the Easter Bunny has been?

Eggs mark the spot.

Where does the Easter Bunny get his eggs?

From eggplants

What does the Easter Bunny get for making a basket?

Two points, just like anyone else.

Why do we paint Easter eggs?

Because it's easier than trying to wallpaper them.

Passover

Why do we have a Haggadah at Passover?

So we can seder right words.

Knock, knock.
Who's there?
Passover.
Passover who?
Passover that kugel to me, please. It smells delicious!

What did the cowboy take to Passover dinner?

A horseradish

Ramadan and Eid

What is the stickiest meal during Ramadan?

Iftar

How do sheep greet each other on Eid?

"Sa-lamb alaikum."

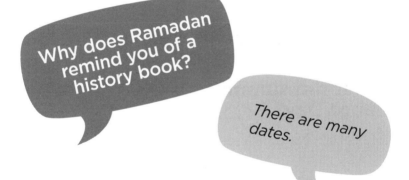

Why does Ramadan remind you of a history book?

There are many dates.

Knock, knock.

Who's there?

Falafel.

Falafel who?

I falafel my bike and hurt my knee.

Memorial Day

What is a cow's favorite holiday?

Moo-*morial day*

How many feet are in a yard?

It depends how many people came to the Memorial Day barbecue.

Labor Day

What did summer say on Labor Day?

"Help! I'm going to fall!"

Diwali

What do birds call Diwali?

The Festival of Flights

> **Why did the gulab jamun win a prize for best dessert?**
>
> *Because it entered a sweet-stakes.*

Knock, knock.

Who's there?

Sherwood.

Sherwood who?

Sherwood like to see some Diwali fireworks!

What do you get when you cross a diya with a volcano?

A lava lamp

Thanksgiving

What is a math teacher's favorite Thanksgiving dessert?

Pumpkin pi

What do astronauts put on their Thanksgiving turkey?

Gravy-ty

What kind of music do Pilgrims listen to?

Plymouth rock

Knock, knock.

Who's there?

Esther.

Esther who?

Esther any more cranberry sauce?

Hanukkah

How long do Hanukkah candles last?

About a wick

What did the loaf of bread say to the other loaf of bread during Hanukkah?

"Happy challah-days!"

What did the dreidel say to the menorah?

"Spin too long since we saw each other."

What is a llama's favorite holiday?

Llama-kkah

HAPPY BIRTHDAY!

Knock, knock.

Who's there?

Doughnut.

Doughnut who?

Doughnut open this until your birthday.

What has wings, a long tail, and wears a bow?

A birthday pheasant

What do you call a birthday party for fleas?

A flea-esta

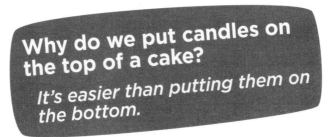

Why do we put candles on the top of a cake?

It's easier than putting them on the bottom.

How can you tell if a hippo's been to your birthday party?

Look for footprints in the ice cream.

Knock, knock.

Who's there?

Raptor.

Raptor who?

Raptor not, your sister will love her birthday present.

What's a birthday candle's favorite state?

Wish-consin

Who did the deer invite to his birthday party?

His nearest and deer-est friends

How do you find out a dinosaur's age?

Go to its birthday party.